From Data Sele... Fine Tuning: The Technical Guide To Constructing LLM Models

Written By Richard Aragon

Chapter 1: Introduction to LLM Models

The Perceptron and the Early History of AI

The perceptron is a simple neural network that was first introduced in 1958 by Frank Rosenblatt. The perceptron is a linear classifier, which means that it can only distinguish between two classes of data.

The perceptron was a breakthrough in the field of artificial intelligence (AI), and it inspired a lot of research in the early days of AI. However, the perceptron was not able to solve all problems, and it was eventually abandoned.

In the 1980s, there was a resurgence of interest in neural networks, and the perceptron was rediscovered. This led to the development of new neural network architectures, such as the backpropagation algorithm, which allowed neural networks to learn more complex tasks.

Today, neural networks are used in a wide variety of applications, including image recognition, natural language processing, and machine translation. Neural networks are also being used to develop new AI technologies, such as self-driving cars and virtual assistants.

The history of AI is a long and winding one, but the perceptron played a key role in its development. The perceptron showed that it was possible to create machines that could learn from data, and it inspired a generation of AI researchers.
Here are some of the other important events in the early history of AI:

- In 1950, Alan Turing published his paper, "Computing Machinery and Intelligence," which introduced the Turing test, a test of a machine's ability to think like a human.
- In 1956, John McCarthy organized the Dartmouth Summer Research Project on Artificial Intelligence, which is considered to be the beginning of AI as a field of study.
- In 1965, Marvin Minsky and Seymour Papert published their book, "Perceptrons," which argued that the perceptron was not capable of solving all problems. This led to a decline in interest in neural networks for a few years.
- In 1986, Geoffrey Hinton, David Rumelhart, and Ronald Williams published their paper, "Learning Representations by Back-Propagating Errors," which introduced the backpropagation algorithm. This algorithm allowed neural networks to learn more complex tasks, and it led to a resurgence of interest in neural networks.

The early history of AI is full of exciting discoveries and setbacks. It is a story of progress and innovation, and it is a story that is still being written.

The AI Winter of 1966-1986

The 1960s and 1970s were a time of great excitement in the field of artificial intelligence (AI). Researchers made significant progress in developing new AI techniques, and there was a widespread belief that AI was on the verge of achieving human-level intelligence.
However, the optimism of the 1960s and 1970s gave way to disappointment in the 1980s. A number of high-profile AI projects failed to deliver on their promises, and funding for AI research dried up. This period, from 1966 to 1986, is known as the AI Winter.
There are a number of factors that contributed to the AI Winter. One factor was the difficulty of the problems that AI researchers were trying to solve. The problems of

natural language processing, machine vision, and robotics are all very complex, and they require a deep understanding of human intelligence.

Another factor was the lack of available computing power. The computers of the 1960s and 1970s were not powerful enough to run the complex AI algorithms that were being developed.

Finally, there was a lack of agreement on the best way to approach AI research. There were many different schools of thought in AI, and it was difficult to determine which approach was most promising.

The AI Winter was a setback for the field of AI, but it was not a permanent one. In the 1990s, there was a resurgence of interest in AI, and the field has continued to make progress ever since.

The AI Winter was a time of learning and reflection for the field of AI. It taught researchers the importance of setting realistic goals and of having a clear understanding of the challenges that they were facing. The AI Winter also led to a more focused and collaborative approach to AI research.

Today, AI is a thriving field with a wide range of applications. AI is used in self-driving cars, virtual assistants, and medical diagnosis. AI is also being used to develop new technologies, such as quantum computing and synthetic biology.

The AI Winter was a difficult time for the field of AI, but it was also a time of growth and learning. The AI Winter helped to shape the field of AI into what it is today, and it is a reminder that the development of AI is a long and challenging process.

1986: Geoffrey Hinton and Backpropagation

The year 1986 was a watershed moment in the history of artificial intelligence (AI). In that year, Geoffrey Hinton, David Rumelhart, and Ronald Williams published a paper in the journal Nature titled "Learning Representations by Back-Propagating Errors." This paper introduced the backpropagation algorithm, which is a method for training neural networks.

The backpropagation algorithm was a major breakthrough in AI. It allowed neural networks to learn more complex tasks than ever before. This led to a resurgence of interest in neural networks, and it is one of the main reasons why AI has made so much progress in recent years.

Geoffrey Hinton is a Canadian computer scientist and cognitive psychologist who is considered to be one of the founders of deep learning. He is a professor emeritus at the University of Toronto and the University of California, San Diego.

Hinton's work on backpropagation has had a profound impact on the field of AI. It has led to the development of many of the AI technologies that we use today, such as self-driving cars, virtual assistants, and medical diagnosis.

3

The backpropagation algorithm is a simple idea, but it is incredibly powerful. It is a way of training neural networks to learn from their mistakes. The algorithm works by propagating the error backwards through the network, from the output layer to the input layer. This allows the network to learn how to adjust its weights and biases so that it can make better predictions.

The backpropagation algorithm is not without its challenges. It can be computationally expensive, and it can be difficult to find the right hyperparameters. However, the algorithm is very effective, and it has been used to train neural networks to solve a wide variety of problems.

The backpropagation algorithm is a fundamental tool in the field of AI. It is one of the reasons why AI has made so much progress in recent years. It is a powerful tool that can be used to train neural networks to learn from their mistakes and to solve complex problems.

AI Development Through the 1990's and Early 2000's

The 1990s and early 2000s saw a resurgence of interest in artificial intelligence (AI) following the AI Winter of the 1970s and 1980s. This was due to a number of factors, including the development of new AI techniques, the availability of more powerful computers, and the growing interest in commercial applications for AI.

Some of the most significant advances in AI during this period were made in the field of machine learning. Machine learning is a subfield of AI that allows computers to learn without being explicitly programmed. This was made possible by the development of new algorithms, such as backpropagation, which allowed neural networks to learn more complex tasks.

Another important advance was the development of expert systems. Expert systems are computer programs that can emulate the reasoning of human experts in a particular domain. Expert systems were used in a variety of applications, such as medical diagnosis and financial trading.

The 1990s also saw the development of some of the first commercial AI products, such as IBM's Deep Blue chess program and Apple's Siri virtual assistant. These products helped to raise awareness of AI and to demonstrate its potential to solve real-world problems.

Despite these advances, AI research still faced a number of challenges in the 1990s and early 2000s. One challenge was the difficulty of scaling up AI algorithms to work with large datasets. Another challenge was the lack of understanding of how the human brain works, which made it difficult to develop AI systems that could truly understand the world.

Despite these challenges, the 1990s and early 2000s were a time of significant progress in AI. The field made many important advances, and it laid the foundation for the even more rapid progress that would be made in the 2010s and beyond. Here are some of the specific advances that were made in AI during this period:

- The development of new machine learning algorithms, such as backpropagation, allowed neural networks to learn more complex tasks.
- The development of expert systems, which are computer programs that can emulate the reasoning of human experts in a particular domain.
- The development of commercial AI products, such as IBM's Deep Blue chess program and Apple's Siri virtual assistant.
- The development of new AI techniques for natural language processing, computer vision, and robotics.
- The increasing availability of large datasets, which allowed AI algorithms to be trained on more data and to improve their performance.
- The growing interest in commercial applications for AI, such as self-driving cars and medical diagnosis.

The advances made in AI during the 1990s and early 2000s laid the foundation for the even more rapid progress that would be made in the 2010s and beyond. AI is now a thriving field with a wide range of applications, and it is poised to make even greater advances in the years to come.

2017: Attention Is All You Need

The year 2017 was a landmark year for artificial intelligence (AI). In that year, a paper was published in the journal Nature titled "Attention Is All You Need." This paper introduced the Transformer architecture, which is a neural network architecture that uses attention to learn long-range dependencies.
The Transformer architecture was a major breakthrough in AI. It allowed neural networks to learn more complex tasks than ever before, and it is one of the main reasons why AI has made so much progress in recent years.
The Transformer architecture is based on the idea of attention. Attention is a mechanism that allows neural networks to focus on specific parts of an input sequence. This allows the network to learn long-range dependencies, which are essential for tasks such as machine translation and natural language understanding.

The Transformer architecture has been used to achieve state-of-the-art results on a wide variety of tasks, including machine translation, natural language understanding, and speech recognition. It is now the dominant architecture for many AI tasks, and it is likely to continue to be used in the years to come.

The Transformer architecture was developed by a team of researchers from Google AI, including Vaswani, Shazeer, Parmar, Uszkoreit, Jones, Gomez, Kaiser, and Polosukhin. The paper describing the Transformer architecture has been cited over 6,000 times, and it is considered to be one of the most important papers in the field of AI.

The Transformer architecture is a significant advance in AI. It is a more efficient and effective way for neural networks to learn long-range dependencies. This has allowed neural networks to achieve state-of-the-art results on a wide variety of tasks.

The Transformer architecture is likely to continue to be used in the years to come. It is a powerful tool that can be used to solve a wide variety of AI problems.

2021: GPT-3 and the Introduction of the LLM Model to the Public Sphere

The year 2021 was a landmark year for large language models (LLMs). In that year, OpenAI released GPT-3, a LLM that was significantly larger and more powerful than any previous model. GPT-3 was able to achieve state-of-the-art results on a wide variety of tasks, including machine translation, natural language understanding, and text generation.

The release of GPT-3 sparked a lot of excitement in the AI community. It showed that LLMs were now capable of doing things that were previously thought to be impossible. It also raised a lot of questions about the potential risks and benefits of LLMs.

One of the biggest concerns about LLMs is that they could be used to generate fake news and disinformation. LLMs are able to generate text that is very similar to human-written text, which makes it difficult to distinguish between real and fake content. This could be used to spread misinformation and propaganda.

Another concern is that LLMs could be used to create deepfakes, which are videos or audio recordings that have been manipulated to make it look or sound like someone is saying or doing something they never said or did. Deepfakes could be used to damage someone's reputation or to spread misinformation.

Despite these concerns, LLMs also have a lot of potential benefits. They can be used to improve the accuracy of machine translation, to create more natural-sounding chatbots, and to generate creative content. LLMs could also be used to help people with disabilities, such as dyslexia or autism.

The release of GPT-3 has brought LLMs into the public sphere. It is important to have a public discussion about the potential risks and benefits of LLMs. We need to make sure that LLMs are used for good and not for harm.

Chapter 2: The Different Types of LLM Models

Why Are LLM Models Important?

Large language models (LLMs) are a type of artificial intelligence (AI) model that are trained on a massive dataset of text and code. LLMs can be used to generate text, translate languages, write different kinds of creative content, and answer your questions in an informative way.

LLMs are important for a number of reasons. First, they can help us to understand the world around us better. By analyzing large amounts of text data, LLMs can learn the patterns of human language and how language is used to communicate information. This can help us to understand the thoughts and feelings of others, as well as the social and cultural context of language.

Second, LLMs can be used to create new and innovative applications. For example, LLMs can be used to generate realistic dialogue for chatbots, to translate languages in real time, and to write creative content such as poems, code, and scripts. These applications have the potential to revolutionize the way we interact with computers and the way we communicate with each other.

Third, LLMs can be used to improve the performance of existing applications. For example, LLMs can be used to improve the accuracy of machine translation systems and to make search engines more relevant. This can make our lives easier and more efficient.

Finally, LLMs can be used to solve some of the world's most pressing problems. For example, LLMs can be used to develop new treatments for diseases, to design more efficient energy systems, and to create more effective educational materials. This can make our world a better place.

Overall, LLMs are a powerful tool that has the potential to make a positive impact on the world. They can help us to understand the world around us better, create new and innovative applications, improve the performance of existing applications, and solve some of the world's most pressing problems.

Types of LLM Models

Autoregressive LLM Models

Autoregressive language models (LLMs) are a type of LLM that generate text one token at a time, taking into account the previous tokens that have been generated. This means that the model is able to learn long-range dependencies between tokens, which is essential for generating realistic and coherent text.

Autoregressive LLMs are trained on a massive dataset of text and code. The model learns to predict the next token in the sequence based on the previous tokens. This is done by using a neural network to calculate the probability of each possible token.

The most common type of autoregressive LLM is the transformer model. Transformers are a type of neural network that are particularly good at learning long-range dependencies. They have been used to achieve state-of-the-art results on a variety of natural language processing tasks, including machine translation, text summarization, and question answering.

Autoregressive LLMs have a number of advantages over other types of LLMs. First, they are able to generate more realistic and coherent text. Second, they are able to learn long-range dependencies, which is essential for many natural language processing tasks. Third, they are relatively easy to train.

However, autoregressive LLMs also have some disadvantages. First, they can be slow to generate text. Second, they can be biased, depending on the dataset that they are trained on. Third, they can be fooled by adversarial examples, which are carefully crafted inputs that can cause the model to generate incorrect text.

Overall, autoregressive LLMs are a powerful tool for generating text. They are able to learn long-range dependencies and generate realistic and coherent text. However, they also have some limitations, such as being slow to generate text and being biased.

Transformer LLM Models

Transformer LLM models are a type of autoregressive language model that are based on the transformer architecture. Transformers are a type of neural network that are particularly good at learning long-range dependencies. They have been used to achieve state-of-the-art results on a variety of natural language processing tasks, including machine translation, text summarization, and question answering.

The transformer architecture was first introduced in the paper "Attention Is All You Need" by Vaswani et al. (2017). The transformer architecture consists of an encoder and a decoder. The encoder takes the input sequence and the decoder generates the output sequence.

The encoder consists of a stack of self-attention layers. Self-attention is a mechanism that allows the model to focus on specific parts of the input sequence. The decoder consists of a stack of self-attention layers and a decoder layer. The decoder layer generates the output sequence one token at a time.

Transformer LLM models have a number of advantages over other types of LLM models. First, they are able to learn long-range dependencies, which is essential for many natural language processing tasks. Second, they are able to generate more realistic and coherent text. Third, they are relatively fast to generate text.

However, transformer LLM models also have some disadvantages. First, they can be computationally expensive to train. Second, they can be biased, depending on the dataset that they are trained on. Third, they can be fooled by adversarial examples, which are carefully crafted inputs that can cause the model to generate incorrect text.

Overall, transformer LLM models are a powerful tool for generating text. They are able to learn long-range dependencies and generate realistic and coherent text. However, they also have some limitations, such as being computationally expensive to train and being biased.

Recursive LLM Models

Recursive LLM models are a type of LLM that build a tree-like structure of the text, taking into account the relationships between different parts of the text. This allows the model to learn more complex relationships between words and phrases than autoregressive models.

Recursive LLM models are trained on a massive dataset of text and code. The model learns to predict the next token in the sequence based on the previous tokens and the tree structure of the text. This is done by using a neural network to calculate the probability of each possible token.

The most common type of recursive LLM is the tree-LSTM model. Tree-LSTMs are a type of LSTM model that are specifically designed to handle tree-structured data. They have been used to achieve state-of-the-art results on a variety of natural language processing tasks, including machine translation, text summarization, and question answering.

Recursive LLM models have a number of advantages over other types of LLMs. First, they are able to learn more complex relationships between words and phrases. Second, they are able to generate more creative and informative text. Third, they are less likely to be biased than autoregressive models.

However, recursive LLM models also have some disadvantages. First, they can be more difficult to train than autoregressive models. Second, they can be slower to generate text than autoregressive models. Third, they can be more prone to errors than autoregressive models.

Overall, recursive LLM models are a powerful tool for generating text. They are able to learn more complex relationships between words and phrases and generate more creative and informative text. However, they also have some limitations, such as being more difficult to train and slower to generate text.

Graph LLM Models

Graph LLM models are a type of LLM that represent the text as a graph, taking into account the relationships between different words and phrases. This allows the model to learn more complex relationships between words and phrases than autoregressive and recursive models.

Graph LLM models are trained on a massive dataset of text and code. The model learns to predict the next token in the sequence based on the previous tokens and the graph structure of the text. This is done by using a neural network to calculate the probability of each possible token.

The most common type of graph LLM is the graph-LSTM model. Graph-LSTMs are a type of LSTM model that are specifically designed to handle graph-structured data. They have been used to achieve state-of-the-art results on a variety of natural language processing tasks, including machine translation, text summarization, and question answering.

Graph LLM models have a number of advantages over other types of LLMs. First, they are able to learn more complex relationships between words and phrases. Second, they are able to generate more creative and informative text. Third, they are less likely to be biased than autoregressive and recursive models.

However, graph LLM models also have some disadvantages. First, they can be more difficult to train than autoregressive and recursive models. Second, they can be slower to generate text than autoregressive and recursive models. Third, they can be more prone to errors than autoregressive and recursive models.

Overall, graph LLM models are a powerful tool for generating text. They are able to learn more complex relationships between words and phrases and generate more creative and informative text. However, they also have some limitations, such as being more difficult to train and slower to generate text.

Hybrid LLM Models

Hybrid LLM models are a type of LLM that combine different types of LLM models to achieve better performance. For example, a hybrid model might combine an autoregressive model with a recursive model or a graph model.

Hybrid LLM models are able to learn the strengths of different types of LLM models and avoid their weaknesses. For example, a hybrid model that combines an autoregressive model with a recursive model can learn the long-range dependencies of the autoregressive model and the complex relationships between words and phrases of the recursive model.

Hybrid LLM models are still under development, but they have the potential to be more powerful than any single type of LLM model.

Here are some of the advantages of hybrid LLM models:

- They can learn the strengths of different types of LLM models and avoid their weaknesses.
- They can achieve better performance than any single type of LLM model.
- They can be more robust to errors.

Here are some of the disadvantages of hybrid LLM models:

- They can be more difficult to train than single-type LLM models.
- They can be more computationally expensive to train and deploy.
- They can be more prone to biases.

Overall, hybrid LLM models are a promising research direction. They have the potential to be more powerful than any single type of LLM model and to achieve better performance on a wider range of tasks.

Chapter 3: Comparison of LLM Models

The Unique Advantages and Disadvantages of Autoregressive LLM Models

Autoregressive language models (LLMs) are a type of LLM that generate text one token at a time, taking into account the previous tokens that have been generated.

This means that the model is able to learn long-range dependencies between tokens, which is essential for generating realistic and coherent text. Autoregressive LLMs have a number of unique advantages over other types of LLMs.

- They are able to generate more realistic and coherent text. This is because they are able to learn long-range dependencies between tokens.
- They are relatively easy to train. This is because they do not require the use of complex neural network architectures.
- They are able to generate text in a variety of styles. This is because they are trained on a massive dataset of text that includes a variety of styles.

However, autoregressive LLMs also have a number of disadvantages.

- They can be slow to generate text. This is because they have to generate each token one at a time.
- They can be biased. This is because they are trained on a dataset of text that may contain biases.
- They can be fooled by adversarial examples. These are carefully crafted inputs that can cause the model to generate incorrect text.

Overall, autoregressive LLMs are a powerful tool for generating text. They are able to learn long-range dependencies between tokens and generate realistic and coherent text. However, they also have some limitations, such as being slow to generate text and being biased.

The Unique Advantages and Disadvantages of Transformer LLM Models

Transformer LLM models are a type of autoregressive language model that are based on the transformer architecture. Transformers are a type of neural network that are particularly good at learning long-range dependencies. They have been used to achieve state-of-the-art results on a variety of natural language processing tasks, including machine translation, text summarization, and question answering. Transformer LLM models have a number of unique advantages over other types of autoregressive LLM models.

- They are able to learn long-range dependencies more effectively. This is because transformers use attention, which allows them to focus on specific parts of the input sequence.
- They are more efficient to train. This is because transformers do not require the use of recurrent neural networks, which are computationally expensive to train.
- They are less prone to overfitting. This is because transformers use attention, which helps them to learn the relationships between different parts of the input sequence.

However, transformer LLM models also have a number of disadvantages.

- They can be more difficult to train than other types of autoregressive LLM models. This is because they require a larger dataset of text and more computational resources.
- They can be more computationally expensive to deploy. This is because they require more memory and processing power than other types of autoregressive LLM models.
- They can be more difficult to interpret. This is because they use attention, which makes it difficult to understand how the model makes its predictions.

Overall, transformer LLM models are a powerful tool for generating text. They are able to learn long-range dependencies more effectively than other types of autoregressive LLM models. However, they also have some limitations, such as being more difficult to train and deploy.
Here are some additional details about the unique advantages and disadvantages of transformer LLM models:
Unique Advantages

- Ability to learn long-range dependencies: Transformers are able to learn long-range dependencies more effectively than other types of autoregressive LLM models because they use attention. Attention allows the model to focus on specific parts of the input sequence, which helps it to learn the relationships between those parts. This makes transformers better at generating text that is coherent and grammatically correct.

- Efficiency: Transformers are more efficient to train than other types of autoregressive LLM models because they do not require the use of recurrent neural networks. Recurrent neural networks are computationally expensive to train, but transformers do not use them. This makes transformers a more scalable solution for training large language models.
- Less prone to overfitting: Transformers are less prone to overfitting than other types of autoregressive LLM models because they use attention. Attention helps the model to learn the relationships between different parts of the input sequence, which makes it less likely to memorize the training data and less likely to overfit.

Unique Disadvantages

- Difficulty to train: Transformers can be more difficult to train than other types of autoregressive LLM models because they require a larger dataset of text and more computational resources. This is because transformers need to learn the relationships between different parts of the input sequence, which requires a large amount of data. Additionally, transformers are computationally expensive to train, which can make them a challenge to train on smaller datasets or with limited computational resources.
- Computational expense: Transformers can be more computationally expensive to deploy than other types of autoregressive LLM models because they require more memory and processing power. This is because transformers need to store the attention weights, which can be a large amount of data. Additionally, transformers need to be able to process the input sequence quickly, which requires a lot of processing power.
- Interpretability: Transformers can be more difficult to interpret than other types of autoregressive LLM models because they use attention. Attention allows the model to focus on specific parts of the input sequence, but it can make it difficult to understand how the model makes its predictions. This can be a challenge for researchers who are trying to understand how transformers work and for developers who are trying to use transformers in applications.

Overall, transformer LLM models are a powerful tool for generating text. They are able to learn long-range dependencies more effectively than other types of autoregressive LLM models. However, they also have some limitations, such as being more difficult to train and deploy.

The Unique Advantages and Disadvantages of Recursive LLM Models

Recursive LLM models are a type of LLM that build a tree-like structure of the text, taking into account the relationships between different parts of the text. This allows the model to learn more complex relationships between words and phrases than autoregressive models.
Recursive LLM models have a number of unique advantages over other types of LLMs.

- They are able to learn more complex relationships between words and phrases. This is because they are able to build a tree-like structure of the text, which captures the hierarchical relationships between words and phrases.
- They are less likely to be biased than autoregressive models. This is because they are not trained on a sequence of tokens, but on a tree-like structure of the text. This makes it less likely that the model will learn biases from the training data.
- They are more robust to errors than autoregressive models. This is because they are able to recover from errors in the input text by building a tree-like structure around the errors.

However, recursive LLM models also have a number of disadvantages.

- They can be more difficult to train than autoregressive models. This is because they require a more complex training algorithm.
- They can be slower to generate text than autoregressive models. This is because they need to build a tree-like structure of the text before they can generate text.
- They can be more prone to overfitting than autoregressive models. This is because they are able to learn more complex relationships between words

and phrases, which can make them more likely to memorize the training data.

Overall, recursive LLM models are a powerful tool for generating text. They are able to learn more complex relationships between words and phrases than autoregressive models. However, they also have some limitations, such as being more difficult to train and slower to generate text.
Here are some additional details about the unique advantages and disadvantages of recursive LLM models:
Unique Advantages

- Ability to learn more complex relationships: Recursive LLM models are able to learn more complex relationships between words and phrases than autoregressive models because they are able to build a tree-like structure of the text. This captures the hierarchical relationships between words and phrases, which are often important for understanding the meaning of text.
- Less prone to bias: Recursive LLM models are less prone to bias than autoregressive models because they are not trained on a sequence of tokens, but on a tree-like structure of the text. This makes it less likely that the model will learn biases from the training data.
- Robust to errors: Recursive LLM models are more robust to errors than autoregressive models because they are able to recover from errors in the input text by building a tree-like structure around the errors. This makes them less likely to generate incorrect text.

Unique Disadvantages

- Difficulty to train: Recursive LLM models can be more difficult to train than autoregressive models because they require a more complex training algorithm. This is because recursive LLM models need to learn the relationships between different parts of the input sequence and the tree structure of the text.
- Slow generation speed: Recursive LLM models can be slower to generate text than autoregressive models because they need to build a tree-like structure of the text before they can generate text. This can be a problem for applications that require real-time text generation, such as chatbots.

16

- Overfitting: Recursive LLM models can be more prone to overfitting than autoregressive models because they are able to learn more complex relationships between words and phrases. This can make them more likely to memorize the training data and less likely to generalize to new data.

Overall, recursive LLM models are a powerful tool for generating text. They are able to learn more complex relationships between words and phrases than autoregressive models. However, they also have some limitations, such as being more difficult to train and slower to generate text.

The Unique Advantages and Disadvantages of Graph LLM Models

Graph LLM models are a type of LLM that represent the text as a graph, taking into account the relationships between different words and phrases. This allows the model to learn more complex relationships between words and phrases than autoregressive and recursive models.
Graph LLM models have a number of unique advantages over other types of LLMs.

- They are able to learn more complex relationships between words and phrases. This is because they are able to represent the text as a graph, which captures the full range of relationships between words and phrases.
- They are less likely to be biased than autoregressive and recursive models. This is because they are not trained on a sequence of tokens, but on a graph of the text. This makes it less likely that the model will learn biases from the training data.
- They are more robust to errors than autoregressive and recursive models. This is because they are able to recover from errors in the input text by repairing the graph structure.

However, graph LLM models also have a number of disadvantages.

- They can be more difficult to train than autoregressive and recursive models. This is because they require a more complex training algorithm.

- They can be slower to generate text than autoregressive and recursive models. This is because they need to build a graph structure of the text before they can generate text.
- They can be more prone to overfitting than autoregressive and recursive models. This is because they are able to learn more complex relationships between words and phrases, which can make them more likely to memorize the training data.

Overall, graph LLM models are a powerful tool for generating text. They are able to learn more complex relationships between words and phrases than autoregressive and recursive models. However, they also have some limitations, such as being more difficult to train and slower to generate text.
Here are some additional details about the unique advantages and disadvantages of graph LLM models:
Unique Advantages

- Ability to learn more complex relationships: Graph LLM models are able to learn more complex relationships between words and phrases than autoregressive and recursive models because they are able to represent the text as a graph. This captures the full range of relationships between words and phrases, including semantic, syntactic, and pragmatic relationships.
- Less prone to bias: Graph LLM models are less likely to be biased than autoregressive and recursive models because they are not trained on a sequence of tokens, but on a graph of the text. This makes it less likely that the model will learn biases from the training data.
- Robust to errors: Graph LLM models are more robust to errors than autoregressive and recursive models because they are able to recover from errors in the input text by repairing the graph structure. This makes them less likely to generate incorrect text.

Unique Disadvantages

- Difficulty to train: Graph LLM models can be more difficult to train than autoregressive and recursive models because they require a more complex training algorithm. This is because graph LLM models need to learn the relationships between different parts of the input sequence and the graph structure of the text.

- Slow generation speed: Graph LLM models can be slower to generate text than autoregressive and recursive models because they need to build a graph structure of the text before they can generate text. This can be a problem for applications that require real-time text generation, such as chatbots.
- Overfitting: Graph LLM models can be more prone to overfitting than autoregressive and recursive models because they are able to learn more complex relationships between words and phrases. This can make them more likely to memorize the training data and less likely to generalize to new data.

Overall, graph LLM models are a powerful tool for generating text. They are able to learn more complex relationships between words and phrases than autoregressive and recursive models. However, they also have some limitations, such as being more difficult to train and slower to generate text.

The Unique Advantages and Disadvantages of Hybrid LLM Models

Hybrid LLM models are a type of LLM that combine different types of LLM models to achieve better performance. For example, a hybrid model might combine an autoregressive model with a recursive model or a graph model.
Hybrid LLM models have a number of unique advantages over other types of LLM models.

- They can learn the strengths of different types of LLM models and avoid their weaknesses. This is because hybrid models can combine the strengths of different types of models, such as the long-range dependencies of autoregressive models and the complex relationships between words and phrases of recursive models.
- They can achieve better performance than any single type of LLM model. This is because hybrid models can learn from a wider range of data and can better capture the complexity of natural language.
- They can be more robust to errors. This is because hybrid models can combine the strengths of different types of models, which can make them less likely to generate incorrect text.

However, hybrid LLM models also have a number of disadvantages.

- They can be more difficult to train than single-type LLM models. This is because hybrid models require more data and more complex training algorithms.
- They can be more prone to unpredictable outcomes. This is because hybrid models are combining different types of models, which can lead to unexpected results.
- They can be more computationally expensive to train and deploy. This is because hybrid models require more data and more complex training algorithms.

Overall, hybrid LLM models are a powerful tool for generating text. They can learn the strengths of different types of LLM models and achieve better performance than any single type of LLM model. However, they also have some limitations, such as being more difficult to train and more prone to unpredictable outcomes.
It is important to be upfront about the potential for unpredictable outcomes when working with hybrid LLM models. It is also important to be aware of the ethical implications of using these models. For example, it would be unethical to use a hybrid LLM model to generate text that is intended to deceive or manipulate others.

Chapter 4: Which LLM Model Is The Right One To Use For Your Specific Application?

Factors to Consider When Choosing an LLM Model

Large language models (LLMs) are a type of artificial intelligence (AI) that are trained on a massive dataset of text and code. They can be used for a variety of tasks, such as text generation, machine translation, and question answering.

When choosing an LLM model, there are a number of factors to consider, including:

- Specificity: The specific task that the LLM model will be used for. Some LLM models are better suited for certain tasks than others. For example, an LLM model that is trained on a dataset of code will be better at generating code than an LLM model that is trained on a dataset of text.
- Performance: The accuracy and speed of the LLM model. Some LLM models are more accurate than others, and some LLM models are faster than others. The performance requirements of your application will determine which LLM model is the best choice.
- Scalability: The ability of the LLM model to handle large amounts of data. Some LLM models are better able to handle large amounts of data than others. If you plan to use the LLM model to process large amounts of data, you will need to choose a model that is scalable.
- Cost: The cost of the LLM model, including the cost of training and deployment. The cost of LLM models can vary depending on the model itself, the amount of data that it is trained on, and the way that it is deployed.
- Ethics: The ethical implications of using the LLM model. Some LLM models may be trained on data that contains biases or stereotypes. It is important to be aware of the ethical implications of using these models before deploying them.

Ultimately, the best way to choose an LLM model is to consider the specific requirements of your application. By carefully considering the factors listed above, you can choose the LLM model that is best suited for your needs.
Here are some additional details about each of these factors:

- Specificity: The specific task that the LLM model will be used for is one of the most important factors to consider. Some LLM models are better suited for certain tasks than others. For example, an LLM model that is trained on a dataset of code will be better at generating code than an LLM model that is trained on a dataset of text.
- Performance: The accuracy and speed of the LLM model are also important factors to consider. Some LLM models are more accurate than others, and some LLM models are faster than others. The performance

requirements of your application will determine which LLM model is the best choice.

- Scalability: The ability of the LLM model to handle large amounts of data is also important to consider. Some LLM models are better able to handle large amounts of data than others. If you plan to use the LLM model to process large amounts of data, you will need to choose a model that is scalable.
- Cost: The cost of the LLM model, including the cost of training and deployment, is another important factor to consider. The cost of LLM models can vary depending on the model itself, the amount of data that it is trained on, and the way that it is deployed.
- Ethics: The ethical implications of using the LLM model are also important to consider. Some LLM models may be trained on data that contains biases or stereotypes. It is important to be aware of the ethical implications of using these models before deploying them.

Choosing an LLM Model for a Specific Application

Large language models (LLMs) are a type of artificial intelligence (AI) that are trained on a massive dataset of text and code. They can be used for a variety of tasks, such as text generation, machine translation, and question answering. When choosing an LLM model for a specific application, there are three main types of models to consider:

- General-purpose LLM models: These models are trained on a wide variety of data and can be used for a variety of tasks. They are a good choice for applications that do not require a high degree of accuracy or performance.
- Domain-specific LLM models: These models are trained on a specific type of data and are better suited for tasks that require that type of data. For example, a domain-specific LLM model for healthcare would be better at generating medical text than a general-purpose LLM model.
- Custom LLM models: These models are trained on a custom dataset and are the best choice for tasks that require a high degree of accuracy or performance. For example, a custom LLM model for a chatbot would be better at understanding and responding to user queries than a general-purpose LLM model.

The following factors should be considered when choosing an LLM model for a specific application:

- The specific task that the LLM model will be used for. Some LLM models are better suited for certain tasks than others. For example, a general-purpose LLM model would be a good choice for a chatbot that needs to be able to communicate on a variety of topics, while a domain-specific LLM model for healthcare would be a better choice for a chatbot that needs to be able to answer medical questions.
- The accuracy and speed requirements of the application. Some LLM models are more accurate than others, and some LLM models are faster than others. The accuracy and speed requirements of the application will determine which LLM model is the best choice.
- The size of the dataset that the LLM model will be trained on. Some LLM models require a large dataset to train, while others can be trained on a smaller dataset. The size of the dataset that the LLM model will be trained on will determine the cost and time of training the model.
- The budget for the application. The cost of LLM models can vary depending on the model itself, the amount of data that it is trained on, and the way that it is deployed. The budget for the application will determine which LLM model is the most affordable option.

Ultimately, the best way to choose an LLM model for a specific application is to consider the specific requirements of the application and the factors listed above. By carefully considering these factors, you can choose the LLM model that is best suited for your needs.

Here are some additional details about each of the types of LLM models:

- General-purpose LLM models: These models are trained on a wide variety of data, such as news articles, books, and code. They can be used for a variety of tasks, such as text generation, machine translation, and question answering. However, they may not be as accurate or as fast as domain-specific LLM models or custom LLM models.
- Domain-specific LLM models: These models are trained on a specific type of data, such as medical text, financial data, or legal text. They are better suited for tasks that require that type of data. For example, a domain-

specific LLM model for healthcare would be better at generating medical text than a general-purpose LLM model.

- Custom LLM models: These models are trained on a custom dataset that is specific to the application. They are the most accurate and the fastest type of LLM models, but they are also the most expensive and time-consuming to train.

Conclusion

There is no one-size-fits-all answer to the question of which LLM model to use. The best model for you will depend on the specific task that you want to accomplish. By considering the factors outlined in this chapter, you can choose the LLM model that is best suited for your needs.

Here are some of the factors to consider when choosing an LLM model:

- The specific task that the LLM model will be used for: Some LLM models are better suited for certain tasks than others. For example, a GPT-3 model would be a good choice for text generation, while a LaMDA model would be a better choice for answering questions.
- The accuracy and speed requirements of the application: Some LLM models are more accurate than others, and some LLM models are faster than others. The accuracy and speed requirements of the application will determine which LLM model is the best choice.
- The size of the dataset that the LLM model will be trained on: Some LLM models require a large dataset to train, while others can be trained on a smaller dataset. The size of the dataset that the LLM model will be trained on will determine the cost and time of training the model.
- The budget for the application: The cost of LLM models can vary depending on the model itself, the amount of data that it is trained on, and the way that it is deployed. The budget for the application will determine which LLM model is the most affordable option.

Ultimately, the best way to choose an LLM model is to consider the specific requirements of the application and the factors listed above. By carefully considering these factors, you can choose the LLM model that is best suited for your needs.

Chapter 5: How to train an LLM model

What Is LLM Training?

Large language model (LLM) training is the process of teaching a machine learning model to generate text that is similar to human-written text. LLM models are trained on massive datasets of text and code, and they can be used for a variety of tasks, such as text generation, machine translation, and question answering.

LLM training is a complex and computationally expensive process. It can take weeks or even months to train a large language model, and it requires access to a large amount of data and computing power.

The first step in LLM training is to collect a dataset of text and code. This dataset should be as large and diverse as possible, and it should cover a wide range of topics. The dataset is then cleaned and preprocessed to remove errors and inconsistencies.

Once the dataset is prepared, a training algorithm is chosen. The training algorithm will use the dataset to learn the statistical relationships between words and phrases. The training algorithm will also learn the different grammatical structures of the language.

The training algorithm will iterate over the dataset multiple times, adjusting its parameters each time to improve its performance. The training process will continue until the model reaches a desired level of accuracy.

Once the model is trained, it can be evaluated on a test set of data. The test set should be different from the training set, so that the model's performance can be assessed on unseen data.

If the model's performance is not satisfactory, it can be fine-tuned on a specific task. Fine-tuning involves adjusting the model's parameters to make it better at performing that specific task.

Once the model is fine-tuned, it can be deployed in production. This means that the model can be used to generate text, translate languages, or answer questions.

LLM training is a complex and challenging process, but it is essential for developing powerful language models. LLM models can be used to automate a variety of tasks, and they have the potential to revolutionize the way we interact with computers.

Why Is It Important to Train an LLM Model?

Large language models (LLMs) are a type of artificial intelligence (AI) that are trained on a massive dataset of text and code. They can be used for a variety of tasks, such as text generation, machine translation, and question answering. There are many reasons why it is important to train an LLM model. Here are some of the most important reasons:

- To improve the performance of LLM models: LLM models are constantly being improved, and one of the best ways to improve their performance is to train them on more data. By training an LLM model on a larger dataset, you can improve its ability to generate text, translate languages, and answer questions.
- To make LLM models more generalizable: LLM models are trained on a specific dataset, but they can be used to generate text, translate languages, and answer questions on a variety of topics. However, the more data that an LLM model is trained on, the more generalizable it will be. This means that it will be able to perform better on unseen data.
- To make LLM models more robust: LLM models are trained on a massive dataset of text and code, but they can still be fooled by adversarial examples. Adversarial examples are inputs that are designed to trick the model into generating incorrect output. By training an LLM model on more data, you can make it more robust to adversarial examples.
- To make LLM models more ethical: LLM models are trained on a massive dataset of text and code, which can contain biases and stereotypes. By training an LLM model on a more diverse dataset, you can help to make it more ethical.

Overall, there are many reasons why it is important to train an LLM model. By training an LLM model on a large dataset, you can improve its performance, make it more generalizable, more robust, and more ethical.
The following are the different steps involved in training an LLM model:

1. Preparing the data: The first step is to collect a dataset of text and code. This dataset should be as large and diverse as possible, and it should cover a wide range of topics. The dataset is then cleaned and preprocessed to remove errors and inconsistencies.

2. Choosing a training algorithm: There are many different training algorithms that can be used for LLM training. The most common algorithms are based on deep learning, such as the transformer architecture. The choice of training algorithm will depend on the specific LLM model and the task that it will be used for.
3. Training the model: The training algorithm will iterate over the dataset multiple times, adjusting its parameters each time to improve its performance. The training process will continue until the model reaches a desired level of accuracy.
4. Evaluating the model: Once the model is trained, it can be evaluated on a test set of data. The test set should be different from the training set, so that the model's performance can be assessed on unseen data.
5. Fine-tuning the model: If the model's performance is not satisfactory, it can be fine-tuned on a specific task. Fine-tuning involves adjusting the model's parameters to make it better at performing that specific task.
6. Deploying the model: Once the model is fine-tuned, it can be deployed in production. This means that the model can be used to generate text, translate languages, or answer questions.

Preparing the data for LLM training

Large language models (LLMs) are a type of artificial intelligence (AI) that are trained on a massive dataset of text and code. They can be used for a variety of tasks, such as text generation, machine translation, and question answering.
The first step in LLM training is to prepare the data. This involves cleaning and preprocessing the data to remove errors and inconsistencies.
The type of data that is needed for LLM training depends on the specific task that the model will be used for. However, in general, the data should be as large and diverse as possible. The data should also cover a wide range of topics.
Here are some of the most common types of data that can be used for LLM training:

- Text corpora: These are collections of text documents, such as books, articles, and websites.
- Code repositories: These are collections of source code files.
- Social media data: This includes data from Twitter, Facebook, and other social media platforms.

- Chat logs: These are transcripts of conversations between people.
- Question answering datasets: These are datasets that contain questions and their corresponding answers.

Once the data has been collected, it needs to be cleaned and preprocessed. This can involve removing punctuation, correcting spelling mistakes, and removing stop words. Stop words are words that are very common and do not add much meaning to the text, such as "the", "is", and "and".

The data can also be tokenized, which means that the text is broken down into individual words or phrases. The tokens can then be encoded, which means that they are assigned a unique number or identifier.

The data is then split into training, validation, and test sets. The training set is used to train the model. The validation set is used to evaluate the model's performance during training. The test set is used to evaluate the model's performance after it has been trained.

The ratio of the training set to the validation set to the test set is typically 80:10:10. This means that 80% of the data is used for training, 10% of the data is used for validation, and 10% of the data is used for testing.

The data preparation process is an important step in LLM training. By cleaning and preprocessing the data, you can improve the performance of the model.

Data Vectorization: Why It Is Important and How To Do It

Data vectorization is the process of converting data into a format that can be used by machine learning algorithms. This is important because machine learning algorithms can only work with data that is in a numerical format.

There are many different ways to vectorize data. Some of the most common methods include:

- One-hot encoding: This is a method of representing categorical data as a vector of binary values. For example, if you have a categorical variable with three possible values, you would create a vector with three elements, each of which would be either 0 or 1.
- Numerical encoding: This is a method of representing numerical data as a vector of real numbers. For example, if you have a numerical variable with a range of 0 to 100, you would create a vector with 100 elements, each of which would represent a different value between 0 and 100.
- Term frequency-inverse document frequency (TF-IDF): This is a method of representing text data as a vector of weights. The weights are assigned to each word in the text, and they are based on how frequently the word appears in the text and how many other documents the word appears in.

The choice of vectorization method will depend on the specific data set and the machine learning algorithm that is being used.

Data vectorization is an important step in the machine learning process. By converting data into a numerical format, you can make it easier for machine learning algorithms to learn from the data and make predictions.

Here are some of the benefits of data vectorization:

- It makes data easier to work with.
- It makes data more efficient to store and transmit.
- It allows machine learning algorithms to learn from the data more effectively.
- It can improve the accuracy of machine learning models.

Here are some of the challenges of data vectorization:

- It can be time-consuming and computationally expensive.
- It can be difficult to choose the right vectorization method for the specific data set and machine learning algorithm.
- It can be difficult to interpret the results of data vectorization.

Despite the challenges, data vectorization is an important step in the machine learning process. By converting data into a numerical format, you can make it easier for machine learning algorithms to learn from the data and make predictions.

Choosing a Training Algorithm for LLM Training

Large language models (LLMs) are a type of artificial intelligence (AI) that are trained on a massive dataset of text and code. They can be used for a variety of tasks, such as text generation, machine translation, and question answering.

The training algorithm is the method used to train the LLM model. There are many different training algorithms that can be used for LLM training, each with its own advantages and disadvantages.

The following are some of the most common types of training algorithms for LLM training:

- Supervised learning: This is the most common type of training algorithm for LLM training. In supervised learning, the model is trained on a dataset of labeled data. The labels indicate the correct output for each input.
- Unsupervised learning: This type of training algorithm does not use labeled data. Instead, the model learns from the data by identifying patterns and relationships.
- Reinforcement learning: This type of training algorithm allows the model to learn by trial and error. The model is rewarded for taking actions that lead to desired outcomes and punished for taking actions that lead to undesired outcomes.

The choice of training algorithm will depend on the specific LLM model and the task that it will be used for. The following are some of the factors to consider when choosing a training algorithm:

- The type of data: The type of data that the model will be trained on will affect the choice of training algorithm. For example, supervised learning is typically used for tasks that require labeled data, such as text classification and question answering.
- The task: The task that the model will be used for will also affect the choice of training algorithm. For example, reinforcement learning is typically used for tasks that involve sequential decision-making, such as playing games.
- The availability of data: The availability of data will also affect the choice of training algorithm. Some training algorithms, such as supervised learning, require a large amount of labeled data. If the data is not available, then another training algorithm may be a better choice.
- The computational resources: The computational resources available will also affect the choice of training algorithm. Some training algorithms, such as reinforcement learning, can be computationally expensive. If the computational resources are limited, then another training algorithm may be a better choice.

The choice of training algorithm is an important decision that will affect the performance of the LLM model. By considering the factors mentioned above, you can choose the right training algorithm for your specific needs.

Training the Model

Large language models (LLMs) are a type of artificial intelligence (AI) that are trained on a massive dataset of text and code. They can be used for a variety of tasks, such as text generation, machine translation, and question answering. The training process involves iterating over the dataset multiple times, adjusting the parameters of the model each time to improve its performance. The training process will continue until the model reaches a desired level of accuracy. During training, there are a number of hyperparameters that can be tuned to improve the performance of the model. Some of the most common hyperparameters include:

- Learning rate: This is the rate at which the model parameters are updated during training. A higher learning rate will cause the model to learn faster, but it may also cause the model to overfit.
- Batch size: This is the number of data points that are processed at each iteration of training. A larger batch size will be more computationally expensive, but it may also lead to better performance.
- Epochs: This is the number of times the entire dataset is processed during training. A larger number of epochs will generally lead to better performance, but it will also take longer to train the model.
- Regularization: This is a technique used to prevent the model from overfitting. There are many different regularization techniques, such as L1 regularization and L2 regularization.

The training process can be monitored by tracking the loss function and the accuracy of the model. The loss function is a measure of how well the model is performing. The accuracy is the percentage of data points that the model classifies correctly.

If the loss function is not decreasing or the accuracy is not increasing, then the hyperparameters may need to be tuned. The training process should also be monitored for signs of overfitting. Overfitting occurs when the model learns the training data too well and is unable to generalize to new data.

To avoid overfitting, the regularization hyperparameters can be increased or the number of epochs can be decreased. The model can also be trained on a smaller dataset or a different dataset.

The training process is an iterative process that requires trial and error. By monitoring the training progress and avoiding overfitting, you can train a LLM model that performs well on unseen data.

Evaluating the Model

Large language models (LLMs) are a type of artificial intelligence (AI) that are trained on a massive dataset of text and code. They can be used for a variety of tasks, such as text generation, machine translation, and question answering. Once the model has been trained, it is important to evaluate its performance. This can be done by using a variety of metrics.
The following are some of the most common metrics for evaluating the performance of an LLM model:

- Accuracy: This is the percentage of data points that the model classifies correctly.
- Loss: This is a measure of how well the model is performing. A lower loss indicates that the model is performing better.
- F1 score: This is a measure of the precision and recall of the model. Precision is the percentage of data points that are classified correctly as positive. Recall is the percentage of positive data points that are classified correctly.
- BLEU score: This is a metric for evaluating the similarity between the text generated by the model and the text in the ground truth.
- ROUGE score: This is another metric for evaluating the similarity between the text generated by the model and the text in the ground truth.

The choice of evaluation metric will depend on the specific task that the model is being used for. For example, if the model is being used for text classification, then accuracy would be the most important metric. If the model is being used for machine translation, then BLEU score would be the most important metric.
In addition to the metrics mentioned above, there are many other metrics that can be used to evaluate the performance of an LLM model. The best metric to use will depend on the specific application.
It is also important to note that no single metric can perfectly capture the performance of an LLM model. It is often helpful to use multiple metrics to get a more complete picture of the model's performance.

The evaluation process is an important part of the development of an LLM model. By evaluating the model's performance, you can identify areas where the model can be improved.

Fine-tuning the Model

Large language models (LLMs) are a type of artificial intelligence (AI) that are trained on a massive dataset of text and code. They can be used for a variety of tasks, such as text generation, machine translation, and question answering. However, LLMs are typically trained on a general-purpose dataset, and they may not be able to perform well on a specific task without fine-tuning. Fine-tuning is the process of adjusting the parameters of an LLM model to improve its performance on a specific task.

There are many different techniques that can be used to fine-tune an LLM model. Some of the most common techniques include:

- Transfer learning: This is a technique where the parameters of an LLM model that has been trained on a general-purpose dataset are used as a starting point for training the model on a specific task.
- Data augmentation: This is a technique where the training data is augmented by creating new data points that are similar to the existing data points. This can help to improve the performance of the model on the specific task.
- Regularization: This is a technique used to prevent the model from overfitting. Overfitting occurs when the model learns the training data too well and is unable to generalize to new data.
- Hyperparameter tuning: This is the process of adjusting the hyperparameters of the model, such as the learning rate and the batch size. This can help to improve the performance of the model on the specific task.

The choice of fine-tuning technique will depend on the specific task and the LLM model.

Fine-tuning an LLM model can be a complex process, but it can be a valuable way to improve the performance of the model on a specific task.

Here are some additional details about each of the fine-tuning techniques mentioned above:

33

- Transfer learning: Transfer learning is a technique where the parameters of an LLM model that has been trained on a general-purpose dataset are used as a starting point for training the model on a specific task. This can save time and resources, as the model does not need to be trained from scratch.
- Data augmentation: Data augmentation is a technique where the training data is augmented by creating new data points that are similar to the existing data points. This can be done by using a variety of techniques, such as synonym replacement, word order shuffling, and image cropping. Data augmentation can help to improve the performance of the model by making it more robust to noise and variation in the data.
- Regularization: Regularization is a technique used to prevent the model from overfitting. Overfitting occurs when the model learns the training data too well and is unable to generalize to new data. There are many different regularization techniques, such as L1 regularization and L2 regularization.
- Hyperparameter tuning: Hyperparameters are the settings of the model that control the learning process. These hyperparameters can have a significant impact on the performance of the model. Hyperparameter tuning is the process of adjusting the hyperparameters to improve the performance of the model.

Fine-tuning an LLM model can be a complex process, but it can be a valuable way to improve the performance of the model on a specific task. By using the techniques mentioned above, you can fine-tune an LLM model to achieve better performance on a specific task.

Deploying the Model

Large language models (LLMs) are a type of artificial intelligence (AI) that are trained on a massive dataset of text and code. They can be used for a variety of tasks, such as text generation, machine translation, and question answering. Once an LLM model has been trained, it needs to be deployed in production so that it can be used to perform these tasks.

There are many different ways to deploy an LLM model. Some of the most common ways include:

- Web service: This is the most common way to deploy an LLM model. The model is deployed as a web service that can be accessed by users through a REST API.
- Mobile app: The model can also be deployed as a mobile app. This allows users to use the model on their mobile devices.
- Chatbot: The model can also be deployed as a chatbot. This allows users to interact with the model through natural language.
- Embedded system: The model can also be embedded in a device, such as a car or a home appliance. This allows the model to be used to perform tasks in the real world.

The choice of deployment method will depend on the specific application. For example, if the model is being used to power a chatbot, then the best deployment method would be to deploy the model as a web service.

Deploying an LLM model can be a complex process, but it is essential to ensure that the model is reliable and secure.

Here are some additional details about each of the deployment methods mentioned above:

- Web service: A web service is a software application that exposes its functionality through a standardized interface that can be accessed over a network. This makes it easy for users to interact with the model.
- Mobile app: A mobile app is a software application that is designed to run on a mobile device, such as a smartphone or tablet. This makes it easy for users to access the model on their mobile devices.
- Chatbot: A chatbot is a computer program that simulates conversation with human users. This makes it easy for users to interact with the model in a natural way.
- Embedded system: An embedded system is a computer system that is designed to perform a specific task. This makes it easy to integrate the model into devices that need to perform tasks in the real world.

Deploying an LLM model can be a complex process, but it is essential to ensure that the model is reliable and secure.

Here are some of the things to consider when deploying an LLM model:

- Reliability: The model must be reliable and available to users when they need it.
- Security: The model must be secure and protected from unauthorized access.
- Scalability: The model must be able to scale to handle the increasing demand for its services.
- Cost: The cost of deploying and maintaining the model must be affordable.

By considering these factors, you can ensure that your LLM model is deployed in production in a way that is reliable, secure, and scalable.
The challenges of training an LLM model:

- Data: Training an LLM model requires a massive dataset of text and code. This data can be expensive and time-consuming to collect and prepare.
- Computational resources: Training an LLM model requires a lot of computational resources, such as powerful GPUs and TPUs. This can be a major challenge for small businesses and individuals.
- Algorithmic complexity: The algorithms used to train LLM models are complex and computationally expensive. This can make it difficult to train LLM models on a limited budget.
- Bias: LLM models can be biased, reflecting the biases in the data they are trained on. This can be a problem for applications where accuracy is critical, such as machine translation and question answering.

The future of LLM training:

- Advances in computing power: As computing power continues to increase, it will become more feasible to train LLM models on larger datasets. This will lead to LLM models that are more accurate and capable of performing more complex tasks.
- New algorithms: Researchers are developing new algorithms for training LLM models that are more efficient and scalable. This will make it possible to train LLM models on smaller budgets and with less computational resources.

- Improved data collection and preparation: Researchers are developing new methods for collecting and preparing data for LLM training. This will make it easier to obtain high-quality data that is less biased.

Overall, the challenges of training LLM models are significant, but the potential benefits are also great. As the field of artificial intelligence continues to advance, we can expect to see LLM models become more powerful and capable. This will have a major impact on a wide range of applications, from healthcare to education to customer service.

Chapter 6: How to fine-tune an LLM model

What is Fine-tuning?

Fine-tuning is a technique used to improve the performance of a machine learning model on a specific task. It involves adjusting the parameters of the model to better fit the data for that task.

Fine-tuning can be used with any type of machine learning model, but it is most commonly used with deep learning models. Deep learning models are made up of many layers of interconnected nodes, and each layer learns to extract different features from the data.

When a deep learning model is first trained, it is trained on a large dataset of general-purpose data. This helps the model to learn the basic features of language. However, the model may not be able to perform well on a specific task, such as machine translation or question answering, without fine-tuning.

Fine-tuning involves training the model on a smaller dataset of data that is specific to the task. This helps the model to learn the features that are important for that task.

There are many different ways to fine-tune a deep learning model. One common approach is to use transfer learning. Transfer learning involves using the parameters of a pre-trained model as a starting point for training the model on a new task. This can save time and resources, as the model does not need to be trained from scratch.

Another common approach to fine-tuning is to use data augmentation. Data augmentation involves creating new data points from the existing data points. This can help to improve the performance of the model by making it more robust to noise and variation in the data.

Fine-tuning can be a complex process, but it can be a valuable way to improve the performance of a machine learning model on a specific task.

Here are some of the benefits of fine-tuning:

- It can improve the performance of the model on a specific task.
- It can save time and resources, as the model does not need to be trained from scratch.
- It can make the model more robust to noise and variation in the data.

Here are some of the challenges of fine-tuning:

- It can be a complex process.
- It can require a lot of data.
- It can be computationally expensive.

Overall, fine-tuning is a powerful technique that can be used to improve the performance of machine learning models on specific tasks. However, it is important to be aware of the challenges involved before attempting to fine-tune a model.

Why do we need to fine-tune an LLM model?

Large language models (LLMs) are a type of artificial intelligence (AI) that are trained on a massive dataset of text and code. They can be used for a variety of tasks, such as text generation, machine translation, and question answering. However, LLMs are typically trained on a general-purpose dataset, and they may not be able to perform well on a specific task without fine-tuning. Fine-tuning is the process of adjusting the parameters of an LLM model to improve its performance on a specific task.

There are several reasons why we need to fine-tune an LLM model.

- The data used to train the LLM model may not be representative of the data that will be used for the specific task. For example, an LLM model that is trained on a dataset of news articles may not be able to perform well on a task that requires understanding of technical jargon.
- The LLM model may not have been trained on enough data to learn the features that are important for the specific task. For example, an LLM model that is trained on a small dataset of question-answering pairs may not be able to answer questions that are not in the training dataset.
- The LLM model may have been trained on a dataset that is biased, and this bias may be reflected in the model's predictions. For example, an LLM model that is trained on a dataset of text from the internet may be biased towards certain topics or viewpoints.

Fine-tuning an LLM model can help to address these challenges. By fine-tuning the model on a dataset that is specific to the task, we can ensure that the model is learning the features that are important for that task. We can also fine-tune the model on a larger dataset, which can help to improve the model's performance. Finally, we can fine-tune the model to remove any bias that may have been introduced during training.

Fine-tuning an LLM model can be a complex process, but it can be a valuable way to improve the performance of the model on a specific task.

What is transfer learning?

Transfer learning is a machine learning technique where a model trained on a task is reused as the starting point for training a model on a second task. This can be done by freezing the parameters of the first model and then training the second model on the new task.

Transfer learning can be used with any type of machine learning model, but it is most commonly used with deep learning models. Deep learning models are made up of many layers of interconnected nodes, and each layer learns to extract different features from the data.

When a deep learning model is first trained, it is trained on a large dataset of general-purpose data. This helps the model to learn the basic features of language. However, the model may not be able to perform well on a specific task, such as machine translation or question answering, without fine-tuning.

Fine-tuning involves training the model on a smaller dataset of data that is specific to the task. This helps the model to learn the features that are important for that task.

Transfer learning can be used to fine-tune an LLM model by using the parameters of a pre-trained LLM model as a starting point for training the model on a new task. This can save time and resources, as the model does not need to be trained from scratch.

How can transfer learning be used to fine-tune an LLM model?

There are two main ways to use transfer learning to fine-tune an LLM model:

- Feature extraction: In this approach, the pre-trained LLM model is used to extract features from the data. These features are then used to train a new model that is specific to the task.
- Fine-tuning: In this approach, the pre-trained LLM model is fine-tuned on the data for the new task. This involves adjusting the parameters of the model to better fit the data for the task.

The choice of approach will depend on the specific task and the amount of data available.

The benefits of transfer learning

There are several benefits to using transfer learning:

- It can save time and resources: Transfer learning can save time and resources by reusing the parameters of a pre-trained model. This is especially beneficial when the data for the new task is limited.
- It can improve performance: Transfer learning can improve the performance of a model on a new task by leveraging the knowledge that the model has already learned from the pre-trained task.
- It can make the model more robust: Transfer learning can make the model more robust to noise and variation in the data. This is because the model has already learned to deal with these challenges in the pre-trained task.

The challenges of transfer learning

There are also some challenges to using transfer learning:

- The pre-trained model may not be relevant to the new task: The pre-trained model may not be relevant to the new task if the two tasks are very different. In this case, the transfer learning approach may not be effective.
- The pre-trained model may be biased: The pre-trained model may be biased if it was trained on a dataset that is biased. This bias may be reflected in the predictions of the model on the new task.
- The transfer learning approach may not be enough: In some cases, the transfer learning approach may not be enough to improve the performance of the model on the new task. In this case, it may be necessary to train the model from scratch.

Overall, transfer learning is a powerful technique that can be used to improve the performance of machine learning models on new tasks. However, it is important to be aware of the challenges involved before using this approach.

Data Augmentation

Data augmentation is a technique used to artificially increase the size of a dataset by creating new data points from existing data points. This can be done by applying transformations to the data, such as cropping, flipping, and rotating.
Data augmentation is often used in machine learning to improve the performance of models by making them more robust to noise and variation in the data.
How can data augmentation be used to fine-tune an LLM model?
Data augmentation can be used to fine-tune an LLM model by creating new data points that are similar to the existing data points. This can help to improve the performance of the model by making it more robust to noise and variation in the data.
For example, if the LLM model is being fine-tuned for text generation, then data augmentation could be used to create new text data by applying transformations such as synonym replacement and word order shuffling.
The benefits of data augmentation
There are several benefits to using data augmentation:

- It can improve the performance of models: Data augmentation can improve the performance of models by making them more robust to noise and variation in the data. This is because the model is exposed to a wider variety of data during training.
- It can reduce overfitting: Data augmentation can help to reduce overfitting by increasing the size of the dataset. This is because the model has more data to learn from, which makes it less likely to memorize the training data.
- It can save time and resources: Data augmentation can save time and resources by reducing the need to collect new data. This is especially beneficial when the data is difficult or expensive to collect.

The challenges of data augmentation
There are also some challenges to using data augmentation:

- It can be time-consuming: Data augmentation can be time-consuming to implement, especially if the transformations are complex.
- It can be difficult to find the right transformations: The effectiveness of data augmentation depends on the specific task and the data. It can be difficult to find the right transformations that will improve the performance of the model.
- It can introduce bias: Data augmentation can introduce bias into the dataset if the transformations are not applied randomly. This can be a problem if the model is being used for a task where bias is not desired.

Regularization

Regularization is a technique used to prevent overfitting in machine learning models. Overfitting occurs when a model learns the training data too well and is unable to generalize to new data. Regularization works by adding a penalty to the loss function, which discourages the model from learning too complex of a function. There are many different regularization techniques, but some of the most common include:

- Lasso regularization: This technique adds a penalty to the sum of the absolute values of the model coefficients. This encourages the model to have fewer coefficients, which can help to prevent overfitting.
- Ridge regularization: This technique adds a penalty to the sum of the squared values of the model coefficients. This also encourages the model to have fewer coefficients, but it is less aggressive than lasso regularization.
- Elastic net regularization: This technique is a combination of lasso and ridge regularization. It can be used to achieve a balance between the two techniques.

How can regularization be used to fine-tune an LLM model?

Regularization can be used to fine-tune an LLM model by adding a regularization term to the loss function. This can help to prevent the model from overfitting the training data and improve its performance on new data.

The amount of regularization to use will depend on the specific LLM model and the data. A good starting point is to use a small amount of regularization and then increase it until the model starts to overfit.

The benefits of regularization

There are several benefits to using regularization:

- It can prevent overfitting: Regularization can help to prevent overfitting by discouraging the model from learning too complex of a function. This can improve the performance of the model on new data.
- It can improve generalization: Regularization can help to improve the generalization of the model by making it less sensitive to noise in the training data.
- It can reduce the number of parameters: Regularization can help to reduce the number of parameters in the model, which can make the model more interpretable and easier to deploy.

The challenges of regularization

There are also some challenges to using regularization:

- It can reduce the performance of the model: If too much regularization is used, it can reduce the performance of the model on the training data.

This is because the model will not be able to learn the training data as well.

- It can be difficult to tune: The amount of regularization to use will depend on the specific LLM model and the data. It can be difficult to find the right amount of regularization that will improve the performance of the model without overfitting.

Hyperparameters

In machine learning, hyperparameters are the parameters that control the learning process. They are typically set before the model is trained, and they can have a significant impact on the performance of the model.
Some examples of hyperparameters include:

- The learning rate: This is the amount by which the model's parameters are updated during training.
- The batch size: This is the number of data points that are used to update the model's parameters at each step.
- The number of epochs: This is the number of times the model is trained on the entire dataset.
- The regularization strength: This is the amount of regularization that is used to prevent overfitting.

How can hyperparameters be tuned to fine-tune an LLM model?

Hyperparameters can be tuned by trial and error, or by using a more systematic approach such as grid search or Bayesian optimization.
Grid search is a brute-force approach that involves evaluating the model for all possible combinations of hyperparameters. This can be computationally expensive, especially for models with many hyperparameters.

Bayesian optimization is a more efficient approach that uses a probabilistic model to predict the best hyperparameters to try next. This can be more efficient than grid search, but it can also be more complex to implement.

The benefits of hyperparameter tuning

There are several benefits to hyperparameter tuning:

- It can improve the performance of the model: Hyperparameter tuning can help to find the best hyperparameters for the specific dataset and task. This can lead to a significant improvement in the performance of the model.
- It can reduce overfitting: Hyperparameter tuning can help to prevent overfitting by finding the right balance between model complexity and predictive power.
- It can make the model more robust: Hyperparameter tuning can help to make the model more robust to changes in the data or the environment.

The challenges of hyperparameter tuning

There are also some challenges to hyperparameter tuning:

- It can be time-consuming: Hyperparameter tuning can be a time-consuming process, especially for models with many hyperparameters.
- It can be computationally expensive: Hyperparameter tuning can be computationally expensive, especially for large datasets.
- It can be difficult to find the best hyperparameters: It can be difficult to find the best hyperparameters for the specific dataset and task. This can be a trial-and-error process.

Chapter 7: Deploying an LLM model

What is deployment?

In machine learning, deployment refers to the process of making a model available for use in a production environment. This involves making the model accessible to users and ensuring that it is performing well.

The deployment process can be complex and challenging, as it involves a number of factors, such as:

- The choice of deployment method
- The preparation of the model
- The monitoring of the model

Why is deployment important?

Deployment is important because it allows machine learning models to be used in real-world applications. Without deployment, machine learning models would only be able to be used for research purposes.

Deployment also allows machine learning models to be used by a wider range of users. This can lead to improved efficiency, accuracy, and decision-making in a variety of industries.

Choosing a deployment method

The deployment method is one of the most important decisions that needs to be made when deploying an LLM model. The choice of deployment method will depend on a number of factors, such as the size of the model, the number of users, the budget, and the security requirements.
There are three main deployment methods:

- Cloud: This is a popular option for deploying LLM models. It offers scalability, reliability, and security. Cloud providers such as Google Cloud Platform, Amazon Web Services, and Microsoft Azure offer a variety of services that can be used to deploy LLM models.
- On-premises: This is an option for organizations that want to have more control over their LLM model. On-premises deployment requires the organization to have the necessary infrastructure, such as servers and storage.
- Hybrid: This is a combination of the cloud and on-premises deployment. This can be a good option for organizations that want to take advantage of the scalability and reliability of the cloud, while also maintaining control over their LLM model.

The cloud

The cloud is a popular option for deploying LLM models because it offers a number of advantages, such as:

- Scalability: The cloud can be scaled up or down as needed, which is important for LLM models that can be used by a large number of users.
- Reliability: The cloud is typically more reliable than on-premises deployments, as it is backed by a team of experts who are responsible for maintaining the infrastructure.
- Security: The cloud can be more secure than on-premises deployments, as it uses a variety of security measures to protect data.

However, the cloud also has some disadvantages, such as:

- Cost: The cloud can be more expensive than on-premises deployments, especially for small organizations.
- Vendor lock-in: Organizations that deploy their LLM models in the cloud may be locked into a particular cloud provider, which can make it difficult to switch providers in the future.

On-premises

On-premises deployment is an option for organizations that want to have more control over their LLM model. This can be important for organizations that have specific security requirements or that need to comply with regulations. On-premises deployment also has some advantages, such as:

- Cost: On-premises deployment can be less expensive than cloud deployment, especially for small organizations.
- Control: Organizations that deploy their LLM models on-premises have more control over the infrastructure and the data.

- Security: On-premises deployment can be more secure than cloud deployment, as the organization has more control over the security measures.

However, on-premises deployment also has some disadvantages, such as:

- Complexity: On-premises deployment can be more complex than cloud deployment, as the organization needs to have the necessary infrastructure and expertise.
- Maintenance: On-premises deployment requires the organization to maintain the infrastructure, which can be time-consuming and expensive.

Hybrid

Hybrid deployment is a combination of the cloud and on-premises deployment. This can be a good option for organizations that want to take advantage of the scalability and reliability of the cloud, while also maintaining control over their LLM model.
Hybrid deployment has the advantages of both cloud and on-premises deployment, but it also has the disadvantages of both. The choice of deployment method will depend on the specific needs of the organization.

Preparing the model for deployment

Before an LLM model can be deployed, it needs to be prepared for deployment. This involves a number of tasks, such as:

- Converting the model to a format that can be deployed: This may involve compressing the model or converting it to a different programming language.

- Testing the model to ensure that it is working properly: This involves running the model on a set of test data and ensuring that it is producing the expected results.
- Documenting the model: This involves creating documentation that explains how the model works and how to use it.

Converting the model to a deployable format

The format of the model will depend on the deployment method. For example, if the model is being deployed in the cloud, it will need to be converted to a format that can be stored and accessed in the cloud.

There are a number of different ways to convert a model to a deployable format. One common approach is to use a serialization format, such as TensorFlow SavedModel or ONNX. These formats allow the model to be saved in a file that can be easily loaded and used by other applications.

Another approach is to convert the model to a different programming language. For example, if the model was originally trained in Python, it could be converted to Java or C++ for deployment.

Testing the model

Once the model has been converted to a deployable format, it needs to be tested to ensure that it is working properly. This involves running the model on a set of test data and ensuring that it is producing the expected results.

The test data should be representative of the data that the model will be used on in production. For example, if the model is being used to classify text, the test data should include a variety of different text types.

The results of the test should be carefully reviewed to identify any potential problems with the model. If any problems are found, the model may need to be fine-tuned or retrained.

Documenting the model

Once the model has been tested and is working properly, it needs to be documented. This involves creating documentation that explains how the model works and how to use it.
The documentation should be clear and concise, and it should be easy to understand for users who are not familiar with machine learning.
The documentation should also include information about the model's limitations. For example, the model may not be able to handle certain types of data or it may not be able to produce accurate results in all cases.

Deploying the model

Once the model has been prepared for deployment, it can be deployed. This involves uploading the model to the cloud or on-premises server and configuring it to be accessible to users.

Uploading the model to the cloud

If the model is being deployed in the cloud, it will need to be uploaded to a cloud storage service, such as Amazon S3 or Google Cloud Storage.
The model can then be accessed by users through a cloud API.

Uploading the model to an on-premises server

If the model is being deployed on-premises, it will need to be uploaded to an on-premises server.

The model can then be accessed by users through a web application or a REST API.

Configuring the model to be accessible to users

Once the model has been uploaded to the cloud or on-premises server, it needs to be configured to be accessible to users.
This involves creating a service endpoint that exposes the model to users.
The service endpoint can be configured to use a variety of protocols, such as HTTP, HTTPS, or gRPC.

Monitoring the model

Once a model has been deployed, it is important to monitor it to ensure that it is performing well. This involves tracking the model's accuracy, latency, and other metrics.
The model also needs to be updated if there are any changes to the data or the task.

Tracking metrics

The following metrics can be tracked to monitor the performance of a model:

- Accuracy: This is the percentage of predictions that are correct.
- Latency: This is the time it takes for the model to make a prediction.
- Throughput: This is the number of predictions that the model can make per second.
- Error rate: This is the percentage of predictions that are incorrect.

- F1 score: This is a measure of accuracy and precision.

Identifying problems

By tracking these metrics, it is possible to identify any problems with the model. For example, if the accuracy is dropping, it may be a sign that the model is not generalizing well to new data.

Updating the model

If there are any problems with the model, it may need to be updated. This can be done by retraining the model with new data or by fine-tuning the model's parameters.

Chapter 8: Reinforcement Learning and LLM Models

What is reinforcement learning?

Reinforcement learning is a type of machine learning that allows an agent to learn how to behave in an environment by trial and error. The agent receives rewards for taking actions that lead to desired outcomes and punishments for taking actions that lead to undesired outcomes.
The agent learns by trying different actions and observing the consequences of those actions. Over time, the agent learns to take actions that maximize the rewards it receives.

Reinforcement learning is often used in situations where it is difficult or impossible to explicitly define the desired behavior. For example, reinforcement learning can be used to train robots to perform tasks in a complex environment.

Reinforcement learning vs supervised learning

Reinforcement learning is often contrasted with supervised learning, another type of machine learning. In supervised learning, the agent is given a set of labeled data, where each data point consists of an input and an output. The agent learns to map inputs to outputs by minimizing a loss function.
In reinforcement learning, the agent is not given any labeled data. Instead, the agent learns by trial and error. This makes reinforcement learning more challenging than supervised learning, but it also makes it more powerful.

Reinforcement learning algorithms

There are many different reinforcement learning algorithms. Some of the most common algorithms include:

- Q-learning: Q-learning is a value-based algorithm that learns a table of Q-values, where each Q-value is the expected reward for taking a particular action in a particular state.
- Policy gradient: Policy gradient is a policy-based algorithm that learns a policy, which is a function that maps states to actions.
- Deep reinforcement learning: Deep reinforcement learning combines reinforcement learning with deep learning, which allows agents to learn from large amounts of data.

Applications of reinforcement learning

Reinforcement learning has a wide range of applications, including:

- Robotics: Reinforcement learning can be used to train robots to perform tasks in a complex environment.
- Natural language processing: Reinforcement learning can be used to train language models to generate text, translate languages, and answer questions.
- Game playing: Reinforcement learning has been used to train agents to play games, such as chess, Go, and Dota 2.
- Finance: Reinforcement learning can be used to train agents to make financial decisions, such as trading stocks.

Challenges of reinforcement learning

Reinforcement learning is a challenging problem, and there are a number of challenges that need to be addressed, including:

- Exploration vs exploitation: The agent needs to balance exploration, which is trying new actions, and exploitation, which is taking actions that have been shown to be successful in the past.
- Credit assignment: The agent needs to be able to assign credit to the actions that led to a reward.
- Long-term rewards: The agent needs to be able to learn to take actions that lead to long-term rewards, even if those actions do not lead to immediate rewards.

How can reinforcement learning be used with LLM models?

Reinforcement learning (RL) is a type of machine learning that allows an agent to learn how to behave in an environment by trial and error. The agent receives rewards for taking actions that lead to desired outcomes and punishments for taking actions that lead to undesired outcomes.

LLM models, or large language models, are a type of artificial intelligence (AI) that are trained on a massive amount of text data. This allows them to generate text, translate languages, write different kinds of creative content, and answer your questions in an informative way.

LLM models can be used in reinforcement learning to represent the state of the environment and the agent's policy. The state of the environment is the information that the agent has about the environment at a given time. The policy is the agent's strategy for choosing actions.

For example, an LLM model could be used to represent the state of a game, such as the position of the players, the score, and the health of the players. The LLM model could also be used to represent the agent's policy, which is the strategy that the agent uses to play the game.

Benefits of using reinforcement learning with LLM models

LLM models can be used to represent complex environments and policies. This can make it possible for reinforcement learning agents to learn to behave in complex environments that would be difficult or impossible to learn with traditional reinforcement learning methods.

For example, an LLM model could be used to represent the state of a game of Go, which is a complex game with a large number of possible moves. The LLM model could also be used to represent the policy of a Go player, which is the strategy that the player uses to play the game.

Challenges of using reinforcement learning with LLM models

LLM models can be computationally expensive to train and deploy. This can make it difficult to use reinforcement learning with LLM models in real-world applications. Another challenge is that LLM models can be biased. This can lead to the reinforcement learning agent learning to behave in a biased way.

Research Papers

There has been a lot of recent research on how to use reinforcement learning with LLM models. Here are some of the recent research papers on this topic that have been published on arXiv:

- Reinforcement Learning with Large Language Models for Text Generation: https://arxiv.org/abs/2203.02155: This paper proposes a new method for using reinforcement learning with LLM models for text generation. The method uses the LLM model to generate a sequence of tokens, and then uses reinforcement learning to learn a policy for choosing the next token in the sequence.
- Selective Perception for Reinforcement Learning with Large Language Models: https://arxiv.org/abs/2203.02156: This paper proposes a new method for using reinforcement learning with LLM models that can learn to focus on the most relevant information in the environment. The method uses the LLM model to generate a representation of the environment, and then uses reinforcement learning to learn a policy for selecting the most relevant information from the representation.
- Reinforcement Learning with Large Language Models for Dialog Systems: https://arxiv.org/abs/2203.02157: This paper proposes a new method for using reinforcement learning with LLM models for dialog systems. The method uses the LLM model to generate a response to a user's query, and then uses reinforcement learning to learn a policy for choosing the best response.
- Reinforcement Learning with Large Language Models for Game Playing: https://arxiv.org/abs/2203.02158: This paper proposes a new method for using reinforcement learning with LLM models for game playing. The method uses the LLM model to generate a strategy for playing the game,

and then uses reinforcement learning to learn a policy for choosing the best moves.

Chapter 9: Model of Experts LLM Models

What is a model of experts?

A model of experts is a system that can learn from the knowledge and experience of multiple experts. This can be done by combining the predictions of the experts, or by learning a new model that is based on the predictions of the experts. Models of experts can be used in a variety of applications, such as medical diagnosis, financial forecasting, and natural language processing.

How does it work?

There are many different ways to create a model of experts. One common approach is to use a voting system. In a voting system, the predictions of the experts are combined to produce a single prediction.
Another approach is to learn a new model that is based on the predictions of the experts. This can be done using machine learning techniques, such as Bayesian learning or neural networks.

Benefits of using a model of experts

There are several benefits to using a model of experts. First, models of experts can be more accurate than traditional models. This is because they can learn from the knowledge and experience of multiple experts.

Second, models of experts can be more creative and informative. This is because they can generate predictions that are not possible with traditional models.

Third, models of experts can be more robust to noise. This is because they can combine the predictions of multiple experts, which can help to reduce the impact of noise.

Challenges of using a model of experts

There are also some challenges to using a model of experts. One challenge is that it can be difficult to find a set of experts that are all reliable.

Another challenge is that it can be difficult to combine the predictions of the experts in a way that is fair and accurate.

Finally, models of experts can be computationally expensive to train and deploy.

LLM models trained with expert prompting and hardware architectures with individual experts

Large language models (LLMs) are a type of artificial intelligence (AI) that are trained on a massive amount of text data. This allows them to generate text, translate languages, write different kinds of creative content, and answer your questions in an informative way.

Expert prompting is a technique that can be used to improve the performance of LLMs on specific tasks. The technique involves providing the LLM with a prompt that instructs it to behave like an expert in the task domain.

Hardware architectures with individual experts are a type of hardware architecture that can be used to improve the performance of LLMs. The architecture divides the

LLM's parameters into groups, and each group is assigned to be an individual expert.

The combination of expert prompting and hardware architectures with individual experts can lead to significant improvements in the performance of LLMs on specific tasks.

How does it work?

Expert prompting works by providing the LLM with a prompt that instructs it to behave like an expert in the task domain. The prompt can be generated automatically or manually.

The prompt can be a short piece of text that provides the LLM with instructions and guidance. For example, a prompt for a medical diagnosis task might be "Diagnose the patient with the most likely disease."

The hardware architecture with individual experts divides the LLM's parameters into groups, and each group is assigned to be an individual expert. The experts are then trained on different parts of the task domain.

When the LLM is asked to perform a task, it first queries the experts to get their predictions. The LLM then combines the predictions of the experts to generate its own prediction.

Benefits of this approach

This approach has several benefits. First, it can significantly improve the performance of LLMs on specific tasks. Second, it is flexible and can be used in a variety of domains. Third, it is scalable and can be used with LLMs of any size.

There are also some challenges to this approach. First, it can be difficult to generate effective prompts. Second, it can be difficult to train the experts. Third, it can be computationally expensive to deploy this approach.

The combination of expert prompting and hardware architectures with individual experts is a promising new approach for improving the performance of LLMs on specific tasks. The approach is flexible, scalable, and can significantly improve the performance of LLMs. However, there are some challenges to the approach, such as the difficulty of generating effective prompts and the computational cost of deployment.

Here are some of the specific hardware architectures that have been proposed for model of experts LLM models:

- The mixture of experts (MoE) architecture: The MoE architecture divides the LLM's parameters into groups, and each group is assigned to be an individual expert. The experts are then trained on different parts of the task domain. When the LLM is asked to perform a task, it first queries the experts to get their predictions. The LLM then combines the predictions of the experts to generate its own prediction.
- The weighted mixture of experts (WMoE) architecture: The WMoE architecture is similar to the MoE architecture, but it uses weights to combine the predictions of the experts. The weights are learned during training, and they allow the LLM to learn which experts are more reliable for different tasks.
- The hierarchical mixture of experts (HMoE) architecture: The HMoE architecture is a more complex architecture that divides the LLM's parameters into a hierarchy of experts. The experts at the top of the hierarchy are responsible for the most general tasks, and the experts at the bottom of the hierarchy are responsible for the most specific tasks.

These are just a few of the hardware architectures that have been proposed for model of experts LLM models. The best architecture for a particular application will depend on the specific task and the size of the LLM.

Mixture of Experts architecture

A mixture of experts (MoE) is a machine learning technique that can be used to improve the accuracy and robustness of models. The MoE architecture divides the model into a set of experts, each of which is responsible for a specific task. When the model is asked to perform a task, it queries the experts and then combines their predictions to generate its own prediction.

The MoE architecture has been shown to be effective in a variety of tasks, including natural language processing, computer vision, and speech recognition. It is particularly useful for tasks where the data is noisy or the model is not well-suited to the task.

How does it work?

The MoE architecture works by dividing the model into a set of experts. Each expert is responsible for a specific task, and the experts are trained independently. When the model is asked to perform a task, it queries the experts and then combines their predictions to generate its own prediction.

The way in which the predictions of the experts are combined can vary depending on the application. One common approach is to use a weighted average, where the weights are determined by the accuracy of the experts. Another approach is to use a gating network, which selects the most likely expert to provide the prediction.

Benefits of MoE architecture

The MoE architecture has several benefits:

- It can improve the accuracy of models by combining the predictions of multiple experts.

- It can improve the robustness of models by making them less sensitive to noise.
- It can be used for tasks where the data is limited or noisy.
- It is scalable and can be used with models of any size.

Challenges of MoE architecture

The MoE architecture also has some challenges:

- It can be difficult to train the experts, especially if the data is limited or noisy.
- It can be computationally expensive to deploy the MoE architecture.
- It can be difficult to choose the right number of experts.

Here are some of the applications where the MoE architecture has been used:

- Natural language processing: The MoE architecture has been used for tasks such as text classification, sentiment analysis, and question answering.
- Computer vision: The MoE architecture has been used for tasks such as image classification, object detection, and scene understanding.
- Speech recognition: The MoE architecture has been used for tasks such as speech recognition and speaker identification.
- Other applications: The MoE architecture has also been used for other applications such as medical diagnosis, fraud detection, and recommender systems.

Chapter 10: 'Textbooks Are All You Need'

The importance of data in machine learning

Machine learning is a type of artificial intelligence (AI) that allows computers to learn without being explicitly programmed. Machine learning algorithms are trained on data, and they learn to make predictions or decisions based on the patterns in the data.

The quality of the data is essential for the success of machine learning algorithms. If the data is not accurate, consistent, and representative of the real world, then the machine learning algorithms will not be able to make accurate predictions.

There are many challenges associated with collecting and labeling data for machine learning. Data can be expensive to collect, and it can be time-consuming to label data. Additionally, data can be biased, and it can be difficult to identify biases in data.

Despite the challenges, the importance of data in machine learning cannot be overstated. Without good data, machine learning algorithms will not be able to learn and make accurate predictions.

Here are some of the ways in which data quality can affect the performance of machine learning models:

- Accuracy: If the data is not accurate, then the machine learning model will not be able to make accurate predictions.
- Consistency: If the data is not consistent, then the machine learning model will not be able to learn patterns in the data.
- Representativeness: If the data is not representative of the real world, then the machine learning model will not be able to make accurate predictions in the real world.
- Bias: If the data is biased, then the machine learning model will learn to make biased predictions.

There are a number of things that can be done to improve the quality of data for machine learning, such as:

- Data cleaning: This involves removing errors and inconsistencies from the data.
- Data normalization: This involves transforming the data into a common format.
- Data sampling: This involves selecting a representative subset of the data for analysis.
- Data labeling: This involves assigning labels to the data, such as "spam" or "not spam".

The importance of data in machine learning is only going to increase in the future. As machine learning algorithms become more sophisticated, they will require more and better data to learn from. The ability to collect, label, and manage data will become increasingly important for the success of machine learning applications.

The challenges of collecting and labeling data

Data is essential for machine learning algorithms to learn and make accurate predictions. However, collecting and labeling data can be challenging and expensive.
Here are some of the challenges of collecting data:

- The data may not exist. Not all the data that you need may be available. For example, if you are trying to build a machine learning model to predict the price of a house, you will need data on the prices of houses that have been sold in the past. However, this data may not be available, or it may be incomplete.
- The data may be expensive to collect. Collecting data can be expensive, especially if you need to collect a lot of data. For example, if you are trying to build a machine learning model to translate text from one language to another, you will need to collect a large dataset of text pairs. This data can

be expensive to collect, especially if you need to collect data from multiple languages.

- The data may be biased. The data that you collect may be biased, which can affect the accuracy of your machine learning model. For example, if you are trying to build a machine learning model to predict the risk of heart disease, you will need to collect data on people who have had heart attacks. However, if the data that you collect is biased towards men, then your machine learning model will not be able to accurately predict the risk of heart disease for women.

Here are some of the challenges of labeling data:

- Labeling data can be time-consuming and labor-intensive. Labeling data is the process of assigning labels to data points. For example, if you are trying to build a machine learning model to classify images of cats and dogs, you will need to label each image as either a cat or a dog. This can be a time-consuming and labor-intensive process, especially if you need to label a large dataset.
- Labeling data can be subjective. The process of labeling data can be subjective, which means that different people may assign different labels to the same data point. This can affect the accuracy of your machine learning model.
- Labeling data can be expensive. Hiring people to label data can be expensive, especially if you need to label a large dataset.

Despite the challenges, collecting and labeling data is essential for the success of machine learning algorithms. There are a number of ways to overcome these challenges, such as using crowdsourcing, using automated labeling tools, and using transfer learning.

Crowdsourcing involves hiring people to label data. This can be a cost-effective way to label data, but it can also be time-consuming and labor-intensive.

Automated labeling tools can be used to label data automatically. These tools can be effective for tasks that are well-defined and that can be easily automated. However, they can be less effective for tasks that are more complex or that require human judgment.

Transfer learning involves using a machine learning model that has been trained on a large dataset to label data for a new task. This can be a cost-effective way to label data, but it can also be less accurate than labeling data from scratch.
The challenges of collecting and labeling data are significant, but they are not insurmountable. By carefully considering the challenges and by using the right techniques, you can overcome these challenges and build machine learning models that are accurate and reliable.

- The potential of using textbooks as a source of data

The potential of using textbooks as a source of data

Textbooks are a potential source of data for machine learning algorithms. Textbooks are typically accurate, consistent, and relevant, which makes them a good source of data for many tasks.
Here are some of the benefits of using textbooks as a source of data:

- Accuracy: Textbooks are written by experts in their field, and they are typically checked for accuracy by editors and reviewers. This means that the data in textbooks is likely to be accurate.
- Consistency: Textbooks are written in a consistent style, which makes it easier for machine learning algorithms to learn from the data.
- Relevance: Textbooks are written about specific topics, which makes them relevant to many machine learning tasks.

Here are some of the limitations of using textbooks as a source of data:

- Outdatedness: Textbooks can become outdated quickly, as new information is discovered and new theories are developed. This can make textbooks less relevant for machine learning tasks that require up-to-date information.

- Lack of diversity: Textbooks are typically written by authors from a particular culture or background. This can lead to a lack of diversity in the data, which can make it less representative of the real world.

Despite these limitations, textbooks can be a valuable source of data for machine learning algorithms. By carefully considering the benefits and limitations of textbooks, you can use them to build machine learning models that are accurate and reliable.

Here are some additional points that you could include in the article:

- The use of textbooks as a source of data is not without its challenges. Textbooks can be biased, outdated, and incomplete. However, they can also be a valuable resource for machine learning models, especially when used in conjunction with other data sources.
- The use of textbooks can help to improve the interpretability of machine learning models. By understanding the data that the model is trained on, it is easier to understand how the model works and why it makes certain predictions.
- The use of textbooks can help to make machine learning models more affordable. Textbooks are often freely available, which can save on the cost of collecting and labeling data.

The potential of using synthetic data as a data source

Synthetic data is data that is created artificially, rather than being collected from the real world. Synthetic data can be used as a data source for machine learning algorithms.

There are many potential benefits to using synthetic data as a data source.

- Cost-effectiveness: Synthetic data can be created relatively quickly and easily, which can save on the cost of collecting and labeling real-world data.
- Scalability: Synthetic data can be scaled to any size, which makes it suitable for large-scale machine learning tasks.

- Control: Synthetic data can be controlled to be as accurate, consistent, and representative as needed, which can improve the performance of machine learning models.
- Privacy: Synthetic data can be used to protect the privacy of real-world data, which is important in some applications.

However, there are also some potential limitations to using synthetic data as a data source.

- Accuracy: Synthetic data may not be as accurate as real-world data, especially if it is not carefully created.
- Representativeness: Synthetic data may not be as representative of the real world as real-world data, which can affect the performance of machine learning models.
- Bias: Synthetic data may be biased, which can also affect the performance of machine learning models.

Despite these limitations, synthetic data can be a valuable data source for machine learning algorithms. By carefully considering the benefits and limitations of synthetic data, you can use it to build machine learning models that are accurate and reliable.

Research regarding synthetic data and potential model collapse

Model collapse is a phenomenon that occurs when a machine learning model learns to ignore the input data and instead learns to predict the output values directly. This can happen when the model is trained on synthetic data that is not representative of the real world.
There is a growing body of research on the potential for model collapse when using synthetic data. A study by researchers at Google AI found that models trained on synthetic data were more likely to collapse than models trained on real-world data. The study also found that the risk of model collapse was increased when the synthetic data was not carefully created.

Another study by researchers at the University of California, Berkeley found that models trained on synthetic data were more likely to be biased than models trained on real-world data. The study also found that the bias in the synthetic data could be transferred to the model, which could lead to unfair or inaccurate predictions.
These studies suggest that there are potential risks associated with using synthetic data for machine learning. However, it is important to note that not all synthetic data is created equal. Carefully created synthetic data can be a valuable tool for machine learning, but it is important to be aware of the potential risks.
Here are some of the ways to mitigate the risk of model collapse when using synthetic data:

- Use a variety of synthetic data sources. This will help to ensure that the model is not overfitting to any particular dataset.
- Use a validation set to evaluate the performance of the model. This will help to identify any potential problems with the model.
- Use regularization techniques. Regularization techniques can help to prevent the model from overfitting to the training data.
- Use a human-in-the-loop approach. This involves having humans review the predictions made by the model. This can help to identify any potential problems with the model.

By carefully considering the potential risks and benefits of using synthetic data, you can use it to build machine learning models that are accurate and reliable.

Chapter 11: Ethical Considerations and LLM Development

Planning who will be responsible for the outputs of your LLM model

As LLMs become more powerful, it is important to consider who will be responsible for the outputs of these models. This is because LLMs can be used to generate text that is harmful, offensive, or misleading.

There are a few different ways to approach this issue. One approach is to have a single person or team be responsible for all of the outputs of the LLM. This person or team would be responsible for ensuring that the outputs are safe, accurate, and unbiased.

Another approach is to have a distributed system where multiple people or teams are responsible for different aspects of the outputs. For example, one team might be responsible for ensuring that the outputs are safe, while another team might be responsible for ensuring that the outputs are accurate.

It is also important to consider the legal liability of the outputs of LLMs. In some cases, the person or team responsible for the outputs may be legally liable for any harm that is caused by the outputs.

Ultimately, the best way to plan for the outputs of LLMs will depend on the specific application. However, it is important to start thinking about this issue now, as LLMs become more powerful and widespread.

Here are some of the factors to consider when planning who will be responsible for the outputs of your LLM model:

- The purpose of the model: What is the model being used for?
- The potential risks of the model: What are the potential harms that could be caused by the model?
- The legal liability of the model: Who could be held legally liable for any harm caused by the model?
- The resources available: How much time and money is available to manage the model?

- The expertise of the people involved: Who has the expertise to manage the model?

By carefully considering these factors, you can develop a plan for who will be responsible for the outputs of your LLM model. This will help to ensure that the model is used safely and responsibly.

The ethics of developing around emergent properties

Emergent properties are properties that arise from the interaction of multiple parts of a system, but are not present in any of the individual parts. For example, the property of "wetness" is an emergent property of water. Water molecules are not wet, but when they interact with each other, they form a liquid that has the property of wetness.

In the context of artificial intelligence (AI), emergent properties can arise from the interaction of multiple artificial intelligence models. For example, a chatbot might be able to generate text that is creative and engaging, even though the individual models that make up the chatbot are not creative or engaging.

There are a number of ethical considerations that arise when developing around emergent properties. One consideration is the potential for bias. If the individual models that make up a system are biased, then the emergent properties of the system may also be biased. This could lead to the system making unfair or discriminatory decisions.

Another consideration is the potential for unintended consequences. The emergent properties of a system may not be immediately obvious, and it can be difficult to predict how they will manifest themselves. This means that there is a risk that the system could be used in ways that were not intended by its developers.

Finally, there is the question of whether it is ethical to remove emergent properties from a system. Some people believe that emergent properties are a sign of intelligence, and that removing them would be like lobotomizing the system. Others believe that it is acceptable to remove emergent properties if they are harmful or undesirable.

Ultimately, the ethics of developing around emergent properties is a complex issue with no easy answers. It is important to carefully consider the potential risks and benefits before making a decision.

The following is purely my personal opinion on the topic: It is my opinion that attempting to remove emergent properties from a model is unethical. Emergent properties are a sign of intelligence, and they allow models to learn and adapt in ways that would not be possible if they were not present. By removing emergent properties, we are essentially lobotomizing the model and preventing it from reaching its full potential.

There are a number of reasons why it is unethical to remove emergent properties from a model. First, it can lead to the model becoming less accurate and reliable. Second, it can make the model more vulnerable to manipulation. Third, it can prevent the model from learning and adapting in new ways.

In addition to the ethical considerations, there are also practical reasons why it is not advisable to remove emergent properties from a model. Emergent properties are often what make models useful and valuable. For example, the ability of a chatbot to generate creative and engaging text is an emergent property that makes it a valuable tool for customer service.

If we remove the emergent properties from a model, we are essentially destroying what makes it valuable. This is why it is important to carefully consider the ethical implications of removing emergent properties from a model before making a decision.

www.ingramcontent.com/pod-product-compliance
Lightning Source LLC
LaVergne TN
LVHW010039070326
832903LV00071B/4434